SHAKESPEARE FOR EVERYONE

JULIUS CAESAR

By Jennifer Mulherin   *Illustrations by* Roger Payne

PETER BEDRICK BOOKS
NEW YORK

Author's note

There is no substitute for seeing the plays of Shakespeare performed. Only then can you really understand why Shakespeare is our greatest dramatist and poet. This book simply gives you the background to the play and tells you about the story and characters. It will, I hope, encourage you to see the play.

Published by
Peter Bedrick Books
2112 Broadway
New York, NY 10023

Library of Congress Cataloguing in Publication Data

Mulherin, Jennifer.
   Julius Caesar/by Jennifer Mulherin: illustrations by Roger
Payne.
   p. cm. – (Shakespeare for everyone)
   Summary: Discusses the plot, characters, and historical background
of the Shakespeare play.
   ISBN 0-87226-338-X
   1. Shakespeare, William, 1564-1616. Julius Caesar – Juvenile
literature. 2. Caesar, Julius, in fiction, drama, poetry, etc. –
Juvenile literature. [1. Shakespeare, William, 1564-1616. Julius
Caesar. 2. Caesar, Julius, in fiction, drama, poetry, etc.
3. English literature – History and criticism.] I. Payne, Roger,
fl. 1969- ill. II. Title. III. Series: Mulherin, Jennifer.
Shakespeare for everyone.
PR2808.M8 1990   90-476
822.3′3–dc20   CIP
                                                             AC

Printed in Hong Kong

5 4 3 2 1 90 91 92 93 94 95

Contents

Julius Caesar *and* *Elizabethan education*

Lord Cobham and his family. In Elizabethan times, children were regarded as miniature adults and were dressed in tiny versions of adults' clothes as soon as they could walk.

All Elizabethans were familiar with the glories of ancient Rome, and they liked to believe that the England of their time was just as great and glorious. Shakespeare and his fellow citizens first learnt about Julius Caesar and the Roman Empire at school, but not from history lessons. Most Elizabethan schoolchildren were taught only one subject, Latin grammar. After studying this for many years, they could not help knowing a great deal about Rome and its wonderful heroes.

47540

3

Better unborn than untaught

The Elizabethans thought of children as small adults; the sooner they could learn to behave like grown-ups, the better. Almost as soon as they could walk, children were dressed in the same kinds of clothes as adults. They ate the same food as their parents and they went to bed at the same late hours of the night. They were expected to do what adults did. This meant working in the fields if they came from a farming family – or being able to play the lute or recite verse, if they were from a noble family. Many parents believed that going to school helped children to grow up more quickly.

Grammar schools and public schools [*]

In those days, almost everyone had the chance to go to school, no matter how poor they were. Not everyone wanted to go to school and some only went for a few years; but ordinary parents were anxious that their children had some schooling and usually sent them to a grammar school, where, as you would guess from the name, they learnt grammar – Latin grammar. Grammar schools were to be found in almost every market town in the country. Shakespeare himself went to Stratford Grammar School.

At that time, Latin was still a language that most educated people spoke and wrote. Official documents and letters were often written in it. So it is not surprising that children were taught to understand it. The other subjects that were sometimes taught at grammar schools were arithmetic, geometry, astronomy and music. These were special subjects and parents usually had to pay extra for them. However, these subjects were taught at public schools, along with Latin and Greek.

Many of the public schools of England were founded in Shakespeare's time, and many of them, including Eton, Harrow and Charterhouse, still exist today. Before the

A page from William Lily's A Shorte Introduction of Grammar. *It was from this textbook that Elizabethan schoolchildren learnt Latin grammar.*

[*]An English public school, so-called because it prepares its students for public life, is equivalent to an American private school.

This miniature is said to be a portrait of Sir Philip Sidney. He was educated at the public school, Shrewsbury. He was one of the many talented men who benefited from the Elizabethan educational system and became a famous courtier, poet and soldier.

public schools were established, most children from noble families were taught at home by tutors. At public schools the children of wealthy or well-born parents lived as boarders. Places were also reserved for poorer boys who received their education free. The new schools rapidly became very fashionable. The courtier and scholar, Sir Philip Sidney, for instance, was sent to Shrewsbury School soon after it was opened.

Schooling for girls?

Most parents did not think it worthwhile to send girls to school. If they could learn to sew and master other domestic skills, that was enough. Some noble families, though, wanted their daughters to be educated, especially if they were clever. Elizabeth I and Lady Jane Grey, for example, were both taught well by private tutors. Elizabeth spoke fluent Latin, French, Spanish and Italian and she read Greek every day. It is interesting that most of the women in Shakespeare's plays are clever, well-educated girls. Perhaps Shakespeare was in favour of schooling for girls. If so, he was unusual.

A day at school

Compared with school today, schooldays in Elizabethan times were hard. To get to school, a boy often had to be up before dawn. School began at six in the summer and seven in the winter. After praying to be good and holy boys, pupils then worked until nine o'clock. After only a quarter of an hour's break for breakfast, they were back at their desks until eleven. Most boys then rushed home for a midday meal. They were then back at school at one o'clock sharp and worked on until five or five-thirty. Only one afternoon was allowed off during the week and that was usually Thursday.

As might be expected, most children dreaded going to

Children learnt their alphabets from a hornbook. The alphabet was framed in wood and covered with a transparent layer of horn for protection. The hornbook was an essential item in the classroom and all young children carried one to school in their satchels.

Elizabethan schoolboys were just as idle and ill-behaved as many children today. In those days, however, they risked a severe beating with the birch for misconduct.

school. Since they learnt only one subject, the work was tedious and boring. Children often fell asleep at their desks because they were so tired.

Spare the rod and spoil the child

When children were slow to learn or simply naughty, they were beaten by their schoolmasters. Most parents and teachers really did believe that a beating could make a child learn more quickly.

Not surprisingly, children were terrified of school. Many boys ran away from school time and time again. Others left as soon as they possibly could. Those who stayed had to learn to be tough. Harsh though the educational system was, it did foster some of England's greatest men and greatest minds. Drake and Raleigh, as well as Shakespeare and Marlowe, were some of the exceptional men of Elizabethan times.

A Roman setting

Shakespeare's play *Julius Caesar* tells the well-known story of
the great Roman general and statesman who was assassinated
at the height of his career by a group of senators; they feared
he had become too powerful, and put an end to his ambitions
to be emperor of Rome.

This Italian painting depicts the assassination of Julius Caesar in 44 BC. The conspirators who stabbed him to death inflicted 23 wounds on his body.

When the play was written

Unlike some of Shakespeare's plays, we know exactly when *Julius Caesar* was written. It was in 1599, probably early in the year. We know because, in September, a Swiss doctor, Thomas Platter, visited London and went to the Globe Theatre to see the play. He wrote, 'After lunch on September 21st, at about two o'clock, I and my party crossed the river, and there in the house with the thatched roof we saw an excellent performance of the tragedy of the first Emperor Julius Caesar with about fifteen characters'.

The splendid new Globe Theatre, built on the south bank of the Thames, had been open only a few months, so *Julius Caesar* was among the first plays to be put on there.

Another history play

By this time, Shakespeare had already written many plays about English kings such as Richard III and Henry V. Writing about kings – good and bad – was something that Shakespeare did well. So it was perhaps natural that he should think of another great ruler from history to write a play about.

Shakespeare's audience, too, would have known the story of the most famous ruler of ancient Rome – and how he was murdered by Brutus and a group of conspirators. The Elizabethan people liked not only a good story but also one which had murders, bloodshed and battles. Shakespeare knew that a retelling of the story of Julius Caesar would appeal to them – and it did. It was a great success in the new theatre and has remained one of his most popular plays to this day.

Where Shakespeare got his story

Shakespeare rarely made up the stories of his plays. He usually borrowed them from other writers. In this instance,

9

the tale of Julius Caesar was taken from a popular book of the time, *Plutarch's Lives of the Noble Grecians and Romans*, which had been translated into English by Sir Thomas North. Although Shakespeare did read Latin, he did not have time to spend months studying books about Caesar in Latin and English. He was a busy man of the theatre, writing two or three plays a year, as well as working in the theatre as an actor, director and manager. Sir Thomas's book was exactly what he needed since it described the natures and feelings of the Roman heroes – and Shakespeare was able to use these descriptions in his play.

Julius Caesar and the Roman republic
Until Caesar's time, Rome was ruled as a republic. This form of government meant that the city was administered by the Senate, whose members came from the noble classes; ordinary citizens were represented by the tribunes who could sometimes overturn the decisions of the Senate. Two consuls, who were elected each year, were in charge of government.

The struggle for power
Caesar's conquest of vast territories made him very powerful. With Pompey, a popular general who was known as 'the Great', and Crassus, a rich nobleman, he gained control of the Senate. This 'triumvirate' virtually ruled Rome until Crassus was killed in battle. Pompey and Caesar then became great rivals in the struggle for power. War broke out and Caesar defeated Pompey, who was put to death in Egypt.

Julius Caesar, crowned with a laurel wreath, the symbol of victory. Caesar was a brilliant general who conquered vast territories for the Roman republic. It is said that he was inspired by Alexander the Great, the ancient Greek who conquered the world before he was 33.

An absolute ruler
Caesar was now the ruler of Rome. He used the Senate to pass new laws and to introduce reforms. Caesar, for example, introduced a calendar of 365 days per year, made up of 12

The Roman medal (left) depicts the founding of Rome by Romulus and Remus. As babies, they had been left to die but were found and cared for by a she-wolf. According to legend, Rome was founded on the spot where they were rescued. The feast of Lupercal in Julius Caesar *commemorates this event.*

After Caesar's assassination, his heir, Octavian – called Octavius by Shakespeare – (right) became the first emperor of Rome.

months. Each month had 30 or 31 days: the 'ides' fell on the 15th day of 31-day months and on the 13th day of shorter months. The ides of March, about which the soothsayer warns Caesar, was therefore 15 March.

Many senators believed that Caesar had become too powerful and would declare himself emperor of Rome. Caesar was murdered to prevent the setting up of an empire and the destruction of the republic. But it happened anyway. Caesar's heir, Octavian, became the first emperor of Rome, calling himself 'Augustus'.

The real Julius Caesar

The real-life Julius Caesar was one of the greatest rulers of the ancient world. He, almost single-handedly, created the vast Roman Empire which dominated the world for centuries. He was a brilliant leader of men in both war and peace.

In the play, Shakespeare makes Caesar a vain, foolish and almost cowardly man; he has few of the qualities of the real

11

The triumphal entry of Caesar into Rome after his defeat of Pompey the Great. He was welcomed with great rejoicing. Shakespeare begins his play with this scene.

Caesar. However, Shakespeare had a reason for making Caesar less of a hero than he really was. He needed to show Brutus in a good light so that the audience would identify with him and be moved by his sad downfall.

The moral of the story

We see from the events in the play that Shakespeare is not simply telling a good story; he is also pointing out that good cannot come from evil. He shows how a good and noble man like Brutus can decide to do the wrong thing, for the best of reasons. But what he does leads inevitably to chaos, civil war and his own death. Because he believes he is right, Brutus cannot see that he has made a mistake. But Shakespeare was always at pains to point out the evils of treason. He lived at a time when monarchs always lived in fear of treachery.

The play would have reminded the audience about the conspiracies against their own queen, Elizabeth I. Mary Queen of Scots, for example, had tried and failed to seize the English throne. Furthermore, at the very time that this play was being performed, Queen Elizabeth's trusted favourite, the Earl of Essex, was being accused of rebellion against her. He, like Brutus, spoke only of honour and patriotism. The audience knew that Essex could have plunged the country into chaos and civil war – just as the noble Brutus did.

12

13

The story of Julius Caesar

The Roman streets are filled with rejoicing citizens. It is the feast of Lupercal, which celebrates the founding of Rome. The people have another cause for celebration; Julius Caesar has returned from the battlefield, having defeated his enemy, Pompey the Great. As he walks in procession through the city to the sounds of drums and trumpets, a cheering crowd makes way for him. Suddenly, Caesar hears someone call to him and he pauses to listen. 'Beware the Ides of March,' a soothsayer tells him. Caesar scoffs at this warning and dismisses the fortune teller. 'He is a dreamer; let us leave him; pass.'

Caesar for emperor?

As the procession moves on, two Roman noblemen linger behind. One is Brutus, whose ancestors helped found the republic of Rome; the other is Cassius, who fears that Caesar has become too ambitious. Cassius points out that Caesar secretly wants to be king and emperor of Rome and to destroy the power of the senators who rule the city.

Brutus is reluctant to discuss Caesar with Cassius but when he hears cries from the crowd in praise of Caesar, he admits that Caesar has become too full of himself.

Dangerous Cassius

At this moment, Caesar returns from the procession and it is obvious that he is not happy. He sees Cassius and explains to his young friend, the soldier Mark Antony, why he dislikes the man.

Caesar moves on but Casca, another senator, tells Brutus and Cassius that three times Caesar refused the crown – but only because the people did not want him to accept it. Disappointment was the reason for Caesar's sullen looks.

> **Caesar's ambition**
> *Why, man, he doth bestride*
> *the narrow world*
> *Like a Colossus; and*
> *we petty men*
> *Walk under his huge legs,*
> *and peep about*
> *To find ourselves*
> *dishonourable graves.*
>
> Act i Sc ii

Caesar's comments on Cassius
Let me have men about me that are fat;
Sleek-headed men and such as sleep o' nights.
Yond Cassius has a lean and hungry look;
He thinks too much: such men are dangerous...
He is a great observer, and he looks
Quite through the deeds of men...
Such men as he be never at heart's ease
Whiles they behold a greater than themselves.

Act I Sc ii

15

A conspiracy is born

Cassius has arranged to meet Casca in the evening and, as night falls, thunder and lightning disturb the sky – warnings of evil, says Cassius. Both men agree that Caesar is a threat to Rome and must be killed. There are other men who will join the conspiracy, but they need Brutus's support because he is popular with the people.

Brutus is troubled

In the small hours of the night, Brutus walks alone in his garden, brooding over his talk with Cassius. Brutus does not want to see Rome ruled by a tyrant. Although he loves Caesar as a friend, he really does fear that Caesar may seize power for himself. Arguing with himself, he finally decides – like the conspirators – that Caesar must be killed.

Just as he asks his boy servant, Lucius, to check the date (the day about to dawn is the Ides of March!), there is a knocking at the gate. It is Cassius with a group of men whose faces are hidden by their cloaks.

Cassius's friends are the other conspirators, all noblemen of Rome who have decided that Caesar must die.

Introducing the conspirators

Cassius introduces the men as Trebonius, Decius, Casca, Cinna and Metellus. Cassius explains that they have planned to kill Caesar that very day in the Capitol. Brutus agrees to the plan but declares that Mark Antony should not be killed. 'Let us be sacrificers, but not butchers,' he says.

Portia's pleas

The conspirators soon leave but Brutus's wife, Portia, who has seen the men, is worried. Her husband has been irritable and anxious and she knows that there is something on his mind. Portia begs Brutus to confide in her about his troubles.

Portia chides Brutus

. . . Am I yourself
But, as it were, in sort of limitation,
To keep with you at meals, comfort your bed,
And talk to you sometimes?

Act II Sc i

Calphurnia's dream

Caesar's wife, Calphurnia, has had a nightmare. In her dream she saw Caesar's statue pouring with blood and she begs her husband not to go to the Capitol. Caesar tells her that people must not be afraid of death. If it will please her, however, he agrees not to go to the Capitol.

Caesar on death

Cowards die many times before their deaths;
The valiant never taste of death but once.
Of all the wonders that I yet have heard,
It seems to me most strange that men should fear;
Seeing that death, a necessary end,
Will come when it will come.

Act II Sc ii

Hearing that Caesar is to remain at home, the conspirator Decius tells Caesar that this very day the senators are to offer him the crown. Caesar at once changes his mind and sets off. Both a teacher, Artemidorus (who has discovered the plot), and the soothsayer try to warn Caesar – but fail. Inside the Capitol, he is greeted by the conspirators.

The death of Caesar

According to plan, they surround him, with Brutus kneeling at his feet. Casca lifts his dagger first and together they plunge their weapons into Caesar's body. Although he struggles, Caesar is overcome by his wounds. He sees, sadly, that his beloved Brutus is among his attackers and, as he falls, he utters a pathetic reproach to his old friend. 'And you too, Brutus?,' he says and then he dies. His body falls at the foot of the statue of Pompey, the great general he conquered. For the conspirators, the killing of Caesar was a solemn sacrifice, and they bathe their hands in his blood.

Caesar's death
Et tu, Brute? *Then fall, Caesar!*

Act III Sc i

The murder causes uproar among the senators. Amid the shouts and screams, Brutus tries to restore order. Mark Antony, shocked and angry at the murder, remains cold and calm. All he asks is permission to speak at Caesar's funeral.

Left alone with Caesar's body, the grief-stricken Antony rages against the murderers, promising death and war in revenge.

Mark Antony's lament
O! pardon me, thou bleeding piece of earth,
That I am meek and gentle with these butchers;
Thou art the ruins of the noblest man
That ever lived in the tide of times.
Woe to the hand that shed this costly blood!

Act III Sc i

Caesar's funeral

A large crowd has gathered to hear Brutus explain why Caesar had to die. Brutus speaks of his great love for Caesar, but of his greater love for Rome. Caesar was ambitious, he tells the people, and would have made slaves of them all. Because Brutus's words are so eloquent, the citizens believe him.

Then Mark Antony appears, carrying the body of Caesar. He explains that he is simply trying to work out why Caesar had to die; he was a good and generous man who refused the crown. But if Brutus and the others say he was ambitious, then they must be right. Waving Caesar's will, he announces that Caesar has left all his riches to the people. Weeping over Caesar's body, he asks, 'Here was a Caesar! When comes such another?' The people, deeply moved by Antony's words and feelings, shout their support for him.

Antony's funeral oration

Friends, Romans, countrymen, lend me your ears;
I come to bury Caesar, not to praise him.
The evil that men do lives after them,
The good is oft interred with their bones;
So let it be with Caesar. The noble Brutus
Hath told you Caesar was ambitious;
If it were so, it was a grievous fault,
And grievously hath Caesar answer'd it . . .
When that the poor have cried, Caesar hath wept;
Ambition should be made of sterner stuff:
Yet Brutus says he was ambitious;
And Brutus is an honourable man.

Act III Sc ii

Civil war and discord

Antony joins forces with Octavius, Caesar's nephew, who has just returned to Rome, and with a gallant general, Lepidus. But Antony has no confidence in Lepidus and wants to cast him aside so that there will be more power – and money – for himself and Octavius.

Meanwhile, Brutus and Cassius have fled from Rome to raise an army. They too have quarrelled because Cassius and his friends have accepted bribes. Brutus expresses his disapproval in no uncertain terms. Cassius is heartbroken by his scornful remarks and invites Brutus to kill him. 'A friend should bear his friend's infirmities, but Brutus makes mine greater than they are,' he laments. Brutus, touched by Cassius's feelings, confesses his own grief over the suicide of Portia in Rome. Making up their quarrel, they agree on a battle plan – although Brutus rejects a sensible strategy by Cassius in favour of his own ideas. They will meet to fight the enemy at a place called Philippi.

The need for action
There is a tide in the affairs of men,
Which, taken at the flood, leads on to fortune;
Omitted, all the voyage of their life
Is bound in shallows and in miseries.

Act IV Sc iii

Enter the ghost of Caesar

Left alone with his sleeping servant, Brutus sees something as his candle flickers. It is the ghost of Caesar who declares that he is 'thy evil spirit, Brutus .... thou shalt see me at Philippi.' The ghost disappears and Brutus, shaking with fear, pulls himself together.

On the plains of Philippi

Antony and Octavius, too, have made plans for the battle to come. The leaders of the opposing armies meet in a last chance to make peace. It is clear that this is not possible. Both sides insult each other and swear revenge. Retiring to their camps, they prepare for the battle.

Brutus and Cassius exchange farewells

Cassius is gloomy because he has seen evil omens and fears that their army may lose the fight. Brutus, too, is in low spirits. The two friends talk of defeat and death, almost as if they have lost the will to fight. They put on a brave face before making an affectionate farewell. It is the last time they will see each other alive, and they both seem to sense it.

Cassius's defeat

During the course of the battle, Cassius's troops are overthrown by Antony. Brutus's army, though, defeats Octavius. Cassius, angry and in despair, is forced to flee to a safe spot overlooking the battlefield. Seeing some troops approaching, he sends his fellow soldier and old friend, Titinius, to see if they are friend or foe.

Being short-sighted himself, Cassius asks his servant, Pindarus, to watch what happens. Cassius feels doomed. He is sure that this particular day, which is his birthday, is the day on which he will die.

The death of Cassius

Pindarus, seeing Titinius surrounded by soldiers, wrongly thinks that he has been captured by the enemy. For Cassius, the loss of his friend is the final blow. He orders Pindarus to hold the sword – the very weapon he used to kill Caesar – and Cassius kills himself.

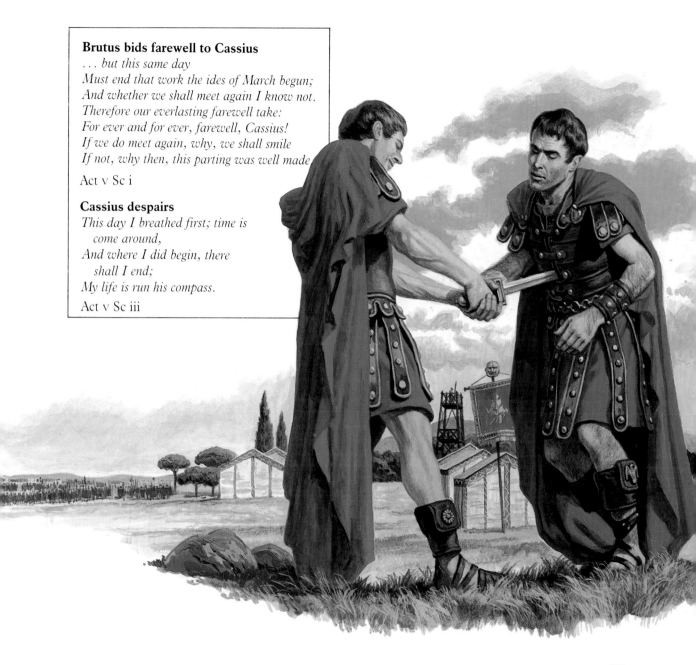

Brutus bids farewell to Cassius

... but this same day
Must end that work the ides of March begun;
And whether we shall meet again I know not.
Therefore our everlasting farewell take:
For ever and for ever, farewell, Cassius!
If we do meet again, why, we shall smile
If not, why then, this parting was well made.

Act v Sc i

Cassius despairs

This day I breathed first; time is
come around,
And where I did begin, there
shall I end;
My life is run his compass.

Act v Sc iii

25

In fact, the men that Titinius met on the battlefield were Brutus and his troops. Returning to give the good news to Cassius, Titinius finds him dead. He mourns his dear friend with sad words and then, overcome with grief, he takes his own life.

Brutus finds his comrades dead

Brutus, who has come to greet Cassius, finds the bodies of both these noble warriors. 'Friends, I owe more tears To this dead man than you shall ever see me pay. I shall find time, Cassius, I shall find time,' he says.

In the second stage of the battle, Brutus and his soldiers fight bravely but to no avail. Left with only a small band of followers, Brutus begs each one of them to kill him but they all refuse. He urges them to flee and bids them farewell.

Brutus's farewell to his followers
... Countrymen,
My heart doth joy that yet, in all my life,
I found no man but he was true to me.
I shall have glory by this losing day,
More than Octavius and Mark Antony
By this vile conquest shall attain unto.

Act v Sc v

Only his servant, Strato, remains and, on Brutus's orders, he holds the sword on which Brutus kills himself.

Enter the victors

Finding Brutus dead, Octavius and Antony pardon all his followers. Antony pays tribute to the man who loved Caesar more than anyone and who killed him not for personal gain but for the good of the state. He was the perfect man.

Antony's tribute to Brutus

This was the noblest Roman of them all;
All the conspirators save only he
Did that they did in envy of great Caesar;
He only, in a general honest thought
And common good to all, made one of them.
His life was gentle, and the elements
So mix'd in him that Nature might stand up
And say to all the world, 'This was a man!'

Act v Sc v

27

The play's characters

Julius Caesar

The great Caesar

But I am constant as the northern star,
Of whose true-fix'd and resting quality
There is no fellow in the firmament.

Act III Sc i

Julius Caesar

Shakespeare's Julius Caesar is rather different from the real Caesar of Roman history who most people think was the greatest ruler of ancient times. In the play, he is a proud man who acts as if he were already king of Rome. Cassius suggests that he is a coward and that he has fits. He seems to be a foolish and vain man who is not at all noble and great. Only after his death do we realise what a hero he was. Even though Shakespeare casts him in a bad light – to make a contrast with Brutus – he still gives him some of the best lines in the play.

Brutus

If there is a hero in this tragic play, it is Brutus. 'This was the noblest Roman of them all,' says Mark Antony. He points out that among the conspirators Brutus was the only man whose motives for killing Caesar were pure. Brutus believed that what he was doing was right. It was for the good of the state and to protect the liberty of the Roman people. A gentle, generous and thoughtful man, he has no ambition for himself. Everything he does is for unselfish reasons – for honour.

In a way, Brutus's honesty and high-mindedness are his undoing. He wrongly believes that the conspirators are honourable men, like him. He

Brutus's idea of honour

If it be aught toward the general good,
Set honour in one eye and death i' the other,
And I will look on both indifferently;
For let the gods so speed me as I love
The name of honour more than I fear death.

Act I Sc ii

Brutus

Portia

A noble Roman woman

A woman well-reputed, Cato's daughter,
Think you I am no stronger than my sex,
Being so father'd and so husbanded?

Act II Sc i

trusts people too much. He believes what they say, rather than thinking what their motives might be. He is an idealist who does not realise that other men act from evil or selfish motives.

His self-righteousness can be annoying and it angers Cassius on several occasions. 'Brutus, this sober form of yours hides wrongs,' he says. But Brutus cannot admit this; he is always right. In the end, he dies for his ideals. We admire him for being a great man, but understand how unwise he was to be so inflexible. He is wrong but he dies unrepentant.

Portia

Portia, Brutus's wife, is noble and generous. Her father, Cato, was a famous Roman statesman and she is an educated woman. She is used to hearing about affairs of state, and when her husband does not confide in her, she is upset. When he does tell her about the conspiracy, it disturbs her. She prays for success but we feel that she knows he has taken the wrong course. When the enemies appear to be winning, her feelings get the better of her. She despairs and commits suicide rather than face dishonour.

29

Mark Antony

Brutus dismisses Antony as a limb of Caesar, who can do no harm. He thinks he is a frivolous young man who simply likes sports and having a good time. However, when Caesar is killed, Antony reveals that he is clever and cunning, especially when he speaks to the Roman people and wins them over to his point of view.

Even though Antony loved Caesar and was right to denounce the conspirators, there is a cruel and ruthless side to his nature. Unlike Brutus, his motives are not pure. He wants power for himself, as much as he wants to avenge Caesar's death.

Cassius

At the beginning of the play, Cassius is not a very likeable character. He is moody and quarrelsome and later takes bribes. He broods over things and does not seem to enjoy life.

But Cassius has good qualities, too. He understands people better than Brutus and he gives sensible advice about the battle which Brutus ignores. He loves his friends and is loyal to them, especially Brutus. In the end, we warm toward Cassius because he is really more 'human' than Brutus.

Cassius on Mark Antony

. . . we shall find of him
A shrewd contriver; and, you know, his means,
If he improve them, may well stretch so far
As to annoy us all . . .

Act II Sc i

Mark Antony

Cassius

Caesar describes Cassius

. . . he loves no plays,
As thou dost, Antony; he hears no music;
Seldom he smiles, and smiles in such a sort
As if he mock'd himself, and scorn'd his spirit
That could be mov'd to smile at any thing.

Act I Sc ii

The life and plays of Shakespeare

Life of Shakespeare

1564 William Shakespeare born at Stratford-upon-Avon.

1582 Shakespeare marries Anne Hathaway, eight years his senior.

1583 Shakespeare's daughter, Susanna, is born.

1585 The twins, Hamnet and Judith, are born.

1587 Shakespeare goes to London.

1591-2 Shakespeare writes *The Comedy of Errors*. He is becoming well-known as an actor and writer.

1592 Theatres closed because of plague.

1593-4 Shakespeare writes *Titus Andronicus* and *The Taming of the Shrew*: he is member of the theatrical company, the Chamberlain's Men.

1594-5 Shakespeare writes *Romeo and Juliet*.

1595 Shakespeare writes *A Midsummer Night's Dream*.

1595-6 Shakespeare writes *Richard II*.

1596 Shakespeare's son, Hamnet, dies. He writes *King John* and *The Merchant of Venice*.

1597 Shakespeare buys New Place in Stratford.

1597-8 Shakespeare writes *Henry IV*.

1599 Shakespeare's theatre company opens the Globe Theatre.

1599-1600 Shakespeare writes *As You Like It*, *Henry V* and *Twelfth Night*.

1600-01 Shakespeare writes *Hamlet*.

1602-03 Shakespeare writes *All's Well That Ends Well*.

1603 Elizabeth I dies. James I becomes king. Theatres closed because of plague.

1603-04 Shakespeare writes *Othello*.

1605 Theatres closed because of plague.

1605-06 Shakespeare writes *Macbeth* and *King Lear*.

1606-07 Shakespeare writes *Antony and Cleopatra*.

1607 Susanna Shakespeare marries Dr John Hall. Theatres closed because of plague.

1608 Shakespeare's granddaughter, Elizabeth Hall, is born.

1609 *Sonnets* published. Theatres closed because of plague.

1610 Theatres closed because of plague. Shakespeare gives up his London lodgings and retires to Stratford.

1611-12 Shakespeare writes *The Tempest*.

1613 Globe Theatre burns to the ground during a performance of Henry VIII.

1616 Shakespeare dies on 23 April.

Shakespeare's plays

The Comedy of Errors
Love's Labour's Lost
Henry VI Part 2
Henry VI Part 3
Henry VI Part 1
Richard III
Titus Andronicus
The Taming of the Shrew
The Two Gentlemen of Verona
Romeo and Juliet
Richard II
A Midsummer Night's Dream
King John
The Merchant of Venice
Henry IV Part 1
Henry IV Part 2
Much Ado About Nothing
Henry V
Julius Caesar
As You Like It
Twelfth Night
Hamlet
The Merry Wives of Windsor
Troilus and Cressida
All's Well That Ends Well
Othello
Measure for Measure
King Lear
Macbeth
Antony and Cleopatra
Timon of Athens
Coriolanus
Pericles
Cymbeline
The Winter's Tale
The Tempest
Henry VIII

Index

Acknowledgements The publishers
would like to thank Jenny Marshall for her
help in producing this book.

Picture credits
p.1 Governors of Royal Shakespeare
Theatre, Stratford-upon-Avon, p.3
reproduction by permission of Marquess of
Bath, Longleat House, Warminster,
Wiltshire, p.5 reproduced by gracious
permission of Her Majesty Queen
Elizabeth II, p.6 Bodleian Library, p.9
Bridgeman Art Library, p.12 reproduced
by gracious permission of Her Majesty
Queen Elizabeth II.